*D*O YOU ENJOY READING other people's mail? The prominent businessman to whom this letter was written invites you to enjoy reading his. He requested information from Bill Bright on how to know God personally. His name has been changed in Dr. Bright's reply, but the message remains the same.

A Great Adventure
Published by
NewLife2000 Publications
Arrowhead Springs 31-00
San Bernardino, CA 92414

©1959, 1992 Campus Crusade for Christ Inc.
Four Spiritual Laws, ©1965.

Printed in the United States of America

ISBN: 1-56399-015-6

Dr. Randolf Van Dusen
Groton Manor
Islip, Long Island, New York

Dear Dr. Van Dusen:

My warm and cordial greetings from
sunny California!

Thank you for your recent kindnesses. I
received your letter this morning and because I sense you have a genuine desire to
know God in a personal way, I am respond-
ing immediately. Your warm expression of
your desire to know more about Jesus Christ
encourages me to explain the basic facts of
the Christian life.

The Christian life is a great adventure.
God loves us and has a wonderful, exciting
plan for us. We are not creatures of chance,
brought into the world for a meaningless,
miserable existence; but rather, we are people

3

of destiny, created for meaningful and joyful lives. Jesus promises, "I have come that they may have life, and have it to the full" (John 10:10).

Since man is the highest form of life, and since there is a purpose for everything else, does it not make sense that God has a plan for us? If God created us for a purpose, does it not logically follow that He has revealed that purpose somehow, somewhere? Would this One who created us then leave us to shift for ourselves? All evidence points to the contrary.

How, then, can we know God's plan? Religion and philosophy have been defined as man's best attempts to find God. Christianity has been defined as God's best effort to find man. Of the eleven major religions in the world today, most have sacred texts that set forth their doctrines. Though these writings may offer some good teachings, they in no way compare with the truths of the Bible, which forms the basis of Christianity. While studying for three years in two of our country's leading theological seminaries under some of the world's greatest scholars, I came to believe conclusively that God has spoken to men in a unique and special way through the writings of the Bible.

Everyone is seeking happiness. Why, then, are more people not experiencing this happiness? According to the Bible, true happiness can be found only through God's way. But we do not naturally follow His way because we are separated from Him. Let me explain.

The Bible says that God is holy and man is sinful. A great chasm exists between them. Man continually tries to reach God through self-effort. Whether a tribesman in the bush country or a professor at a prestigious university, man attempts to close the gap between himself and God. Through various philosophies and religious practices, he hopes to find God and experience a life of purpose and happiness.

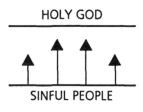

HOLY GOD

SINFUL PEOPLE

In spite of man's desires, he can no more bridge the chasm between himself and God than he can jump across the Grand Canyon or climb to heaven on a step ladder. God created man to have fellowship with Him, but because of his own stubborn self-will and disobedience, man chose to go his own independent way. As a result, his fellowship with God was broken. The Bible calls this sin.

If we pull the plug of a floor lamp out of its wall socket, contact with the electrical current is broken and the light goes out. This illustrates what happens to man when fellowship with God is broken. The Bible says, "All have sinned and fall short of the glory of God" (Romans 3:23) and "The wages of sin is death" (Romans 6:23).

I am not saying that sin is a matter of getting drunk, committing murder, or being immoral. These are only the results of sin. You may ask, "What are the symptoms of a life separated from God?" Besides the more obvious sins, other evidences are worry, irritability, frustration, lack of purpose, inferiority complex, the desire to escape reality, and the fear of death. These and many other

6

evidences show that man is cut off from the only One who can give him the power to live the abundant life.

St. Augustine, one of the greatest philosophers of all time, said, "You have made us for Yourself, O God, and our hearts are restless until they find their rest in You." Pascal, the great physicist and philosopher, described the longing in the human heart this way: "There was once in man a true happiness of which there now remain only the mark and empty trace which he in vain tries to fill from all his surroundings. But these are all inadequate because the infinite abyss can only be filled by God Himself."

Now if God has a plan for us, which includes a full and abundant life, and all of man's efforts to find God are futile, we must turn to the Bible to see God's way. The Bible says, "God so loved the world that he gave his one and only Son, that whoever believes in Him shall not perish but have eternal life" (John 3:16).

In other words, the great chasm between God and us cannot be bridged by our effort, but only by God through His Son, Jesus

Christ. We cannot reach God through good works. The apostle Paul writes, "By grace you have been saved, through faith—and this not from yourselves, it is the gift of God—not by works, so that no one can boast" (Ephesians 2:8,9). Good works will follow as an expression of our gratitude when we accept God's gift of eternal life through Jesus Christ.

Who is Jesus Christ that He, more than anyone who has ever lived, has the power to bridge the chasm between a holy God and sinful man?

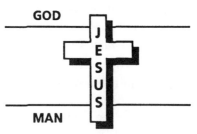

Jesus of Nazareth, conceived by the Holy Spirit, was born to the Virgin Mary almost 2,000 years ago. Hundreds of years before, great prophets of Israel foretold His coming. The Old Testament, written by many individuals over a period of 1,500

years, contains more than three hundred references to His coming. At the age of 30, Jesus began His public ministry. In the following three years, He gave man the formula for a full and abundant life here on earth, and for a life to come. The life He led, the miracles He performed, the words He spoke, His death on the cross, His resurrection, His ascent to heaven, all point to the fact that He was not a mere man.

Arnold Toynbee, the eminent historian, gave more space in his writings to Jesus of Nazareth than to any of the other great men who ever lived including Mohammed, Buddha, Caesar, Napoleon and George Washington. The *Encyclopedia Britannica* gives 20,000 words to Jesus. Thinking men of all nations and religions, who have investigated the evidence, agree that Jesus is the greatest personality the world has ever known.

Jesus Christ claimed to be God. He said, "I and the Father are one" (John 10:30) and "Anyone who has seen me has seen the Father" (John 14:9). He claimed to be the author of a new way of life. Jesus said, "I am the way and the truth and the life. No one comes to the Father except through me" (John 14:6). Historically, we know that wherever His message has gone, new life, new hope and new purpose for living have resulted.

Either Jesus of Nazareth was who He claimed to be—the Son of God, the Savior of mankind—or He was the greatest impostor the world has ever known. If His claims were false, more good has resulted from a lie than has ever been accomplished by the truth. Does it not make sense that He (whom most people knowing the facts consider the greatest teacher, the greatest example, the greatest leader the world has ever known) would be (as He Himself claimed to be, and as the Bible tells that He is) the one person who could bridge the chasm between God and man?

Romans 6:23 says, "The wages of sin is death, but the gift of God is eternal life in Christ Jesus our Lord." As you study the religions and philosophies of the world, you will find no provision for man's sin that is acceptable to God apart from the cross of Jesus Christ. The Bible says that without the shedding of blood there is no forgiveness of sin.[1] In Acts 4:12, Luke writes, "Salvation is found in no one else, for there is no other name under heaven given to men by which we must be saved."

Jesus, in His own words, tells us what we must do to receive eternal life. Let me quote to you what He said to a man who came to Him for counsel. They talked, even as we have talked. Turn to the third chapter of John's Gospel and read the first eight verses.

First, notice who Nicodemus was. He was a Pharisee, a ruler of the Jews, one of the great religious leaders of his day. So far as the law was concerned, he was above reproach. He was moral and ethical. Tradition tells us he was so eager to please God that he prayed seven times a day. He went to the synagogue to worship God three times a day. Yet he saw in the life of Jesus something which he had never experienced himself, a different quality of life altogether.

You will note that Nicodemus approached Jesus by saying, "Rabbi, we know you are a teacher who has come from God.

For no one could perform the miraculous signs you are doing if God were not with him."

In reply Jesus declared, "I tell you the truth, no one can see the kingdom of God unless he is born again."

"How can a man be born when he is old?" Nicodemus asked. "Surely he cannot enter a second time into his mother's womb to be born!"

Jesus answered, "I tell you the truth, no one can enter the kingdom of God unless he is born of water and the Spirit. Flesh gives birth to flesh, but the Spirit gives birth to spirit. You should not be surprised at my saying, 'You must be born again.'"

Let me illustrate this truth. Consider a caterpillar crawling in the dust. One day this ugly, hairy worm weaves a cocoon around its body. From this cocoon emerges a beautiful butterfly. We do not understand fully what takes place. We realize only that where once a worm crawled in the dust, now a butterfly soars through the sky. A similar transformation takes place in our lives as we experience the new birth. Where once we lived on the lowest level as sinful, egocentric individuals, we now dwell on the highest plane, experiencing full and abundant lives as children of God.

We become Christians through a spiritual birth. God is Spirit and without His indwelling presence, we cannot communicate with Him. Therefore, we know nothing of His plan for us. The Bible seems to be a dull, irrelevant book.

However, when Jesus comes into our lives and we surrender to His lordship, we become Spirit-controlled: we love to be with Christians, we love to read the Word of God, and we want our lives to count for Him.

Suppose we are sitting in a room paging through a TV guide. We know that there are a number of television programs available to us. However, we cannot get access to television programs while the TV set is off. The moment we turn on the television and select a channel, we can hear a voice and see a picture. So it is when Christ comes into our lives. He is our divine instrument, tuning us in to God, making known God's will and love for our lives.

I remember well that night years ago when, alone in my room, I knelt to surrender my will to Christ. I must confess that I felt no great emotional response, as some have. But true to His promise, Christ came in; and gradually, like the blooming of a lovely rose, the beauty and fragrance of His presence became real to me. Although I thought I was perfectly happy and challenged with life as a nonbeliever, Jesus gave me a new quality of life altogether—an abundant life fulfilled in ways too numerous to mention.

God loves you so much that He gave His only begotten Son to die on the cross for your sins; and Jesus Christ, the Son of God, loved you enough to die on the cross for you. Here He is, the greatest leader, the greatest teacher, the greatest example the world has ever known. But more than this, He is your Savior. Can you think of anyone whom you would rather follow?

Perhaps you are asking, "Suppose I invite Christ into my life and nothing happens? Maybe He will not hear me."

Jesus says, "Here I am! I stand at the door, and knock. If anyone hears my voice and opens the door, I will come in" (Revelation 3:20). I assure you that you can trust Him to do what He promises. He does not lie.

Any student knows that there are definite laws in the physical realm. A chemist going into a laboratory to perform an experiment knows that by following the Table of Chemical Valence he will get the desired results. In making calculations, the mathematician knows that he can depend upon the accuracy of the multiplication table, and we all know that the law of gravity cannot be violated. Just so, there are definite spiritual laws that govern our spiritual lives. When God, who created all things and established the laws that govern all things, says that He will enter and change your life, you may accept this promise without question.

Our lives are filled with many activities, such as business, travel, finances, social and family interests. Jesus knocks at the door of our heart seeking entrance. But He will not force Himself.

Basically, the only thing that separates us from God—and thus from His love and forgiveness—is our own self-will. (Please do not think me presumptuous. I do not wish to embarrass you by encouraging you to do anything that you are reluctant to do. However, because you expressed such genuine interest in knowing more about these matters when we talked face to face, I am taking the liberty, as one who sincerely cares, by encouraging you to enter into this relationship with Christ today—now!)

Jesus says, "My purpose is to give life in all its fullness" (John 10:10, TLB). Jesus wants to come into your life and make harmony out of discord. He wants to create meaning in your life in place of emptiness. He wants to forgive your sin and bridge the gulf between you and God. Jesus does not want to enter your life as a guest, but He wants to control your life as Lord and Master.

Let me illustrate.

SELF-DIRECTED LIFE

S—Self is on the throne

†—Christ is outside the life

●—Interests are directed by self, often resulting in discord and frustration

16

The circle represents your life, and the throne represents your control center or will. All of these years, your ego has been on the throne. Your interests have been controlled by self, often resulting in discord and frustration. Christ is waiting for you to step down and relinquish the authority of your life to Him so that He can occupy the throne.

CHRIST-DIRECTED LIFE

†—Christ is in the life and on the throne
S—Self is yielding to Christ
•—Interests are directed by Christ, resulting in harmony with God's plan

You can see from this simple diagram that when Christ becomes Lord of your life, He becomes Lord of every activity. This results in a harmonious life. Is it not better to invite an all-powerful, loving God who created you and suffered for you to direct your life than to rely on yourself?

The Bible tells us that "God has given us eternal life, and this life is in his Son. He who has the Son has life; he who does not have the Son of God does not have life" (1 John

5:11,12, NASB). In John 1:12, we are told, "To all who received him, to those who believed in his name, he gave the right to become children of God."

Will you sincerely invite the Lord Jesus into your heart, and surrender your life completely to Him, right now? To invite Christ into your life is the most important decision you will ever make. When you do, several wonderful things happen:

1. Christ comes to live in your heart.
2. He forgives all your sins.
3. You become a child of God.
4. You receive eternal life.
5. God will reveal His plan and purpose for your life.

Find a quiet place where you can kneel or bow reverently in God's presence and ask Christ to come into your heart. Pray in your own words. God knows your heart and is not concerned with your words but rather with the attitude of your heart. In your prayer, you can say something like this:

Lord Jesus, I need you. I want to know You personally. Thank You for

*dying on the cross for my sins. I open
the door of my life and receive You as
my Savior and Lord. Thank You for
forgiving my sins and giving me
eternal life. Take control of the throne
of my life. Make me the kind of person
You want me to be.*

Did you ask Christ into your heart? If you
prayed this prayer sincerely, you can rejoice
that Jesus forgave your sins and entered into
your life. This means that your slate is clean
and you are starting over. The Bible says, "If
anyone is in Christ, he is a new creation; the
old has gone, the new has come!" (2
Corinthians 5:17).

Do not be disappointed if you have not
had a great emotional experience—though
some have indeed known this immediate
joy. A Christian must place his faith in the
Word of God, not in feelings; emotions
come and go, but the Word of God is
trustworthy and true.

Christ promised to enter when you
opened the door. You never need to ask
Jesus into your life again—for He promised never to leave or forsake you. Daily

acknowledge Him as your Lord and invite Him to live and love through you each moment of every day the rest of your life. Meditate again on the truth of Revelation 3:20, John 1:12, 1 John 5:11,12, and 2 Corinthians 5:17. Take time right now to thank God for what happened to you as you prayed.

Since you have never been satisfied with mediocrity in your business, Dr. Van Dusen, you will certainly not want to be an ordinary Christian. It costs us nothing to become Christians, though it cost God His own dear Son to give us this privilege. But it requires both time and discipline to mature as a Christian.

Let me suggest several things that you can do to grow quickly in your Christian life. This simple word will help you remember them—GROW:

G   Go to God in prayer daily.

R   Read God's Word every day. Begin with the Gospel of John.

O   Obey God moment by moment.

W   Witness for Christ by your life and words.

20

Attending church regularly is a vital part of growing in Christ. Hebrews 10:25 counsels, "Let us not give up meeting together, as some are in the habit of doing, but let us encourage one another." Let me illustrate. Several logs burn brightly together. Put one aside on the cold hearth and the fire goes out. So it is with you and your relationship to other Christians. If you do not belong to a church, do not wait for someone to invite you. Take the initiative. Call the pastor of a nearby church where Christ is honored and the Bible is preached. Make plans to start next Sunday and to attend each week.

Be assured of my love and prayers. I will be looking forward to hearing from you soon.

Sincerely yours,

William R. Bright
President
WRB:br

Perhaps you have invited Christ into your life as a result of reading this book. I have a series of booklets called *Transferable Concepts* that can help you grow in your Christian life.

Transferable Concepts are ideal for individual and group study. You can request copies of these booklets and other resources by completing the Response Form at the back of this book.

As you read *A Great Adventure,* you may have noticed that there are some basic principles involved in developing a personal relationship with God. *The Four Spiritual Laws,* found in the next few pages, explain these principles more fully.

HAVE YOU HEARD
OF THE
FOUR SPIRITUAL LAWS?

Just as there are physical laws that govern the physical universe, so are there spiritual laws which govern your relationship with God.

LAW ONE

GOD **LOVES** YOU AND HAS A WONDERFUL **PLAN** FOR YOUR LIFE.

God's Love

"God so loved the world, that He gave His only begotten Son, that whoever believes in Him should not perish, but have eternal life" (John 3:16, NASB).

God's Plan

(Christ speaking) "I came that they might have life, and might have it abundantly" [that it might be full and meaningful] (John 10:10, NASB).

Why is it that most people are not experiencing the abundant life?

Because...

23

LAW TWO

MAN IS **SINFUL** AND **SEPARATED** FROM GOD, THUS HE CANNOT KNOW AND EXPERIENCE GOD'S LOVE AND PLAN FOR HIS LIFE.

Man Is Sinful

"All have sinned and fall short of the glory of God" (Romans 3:23, NASB).

Man was created to have fellowship with God; but, because of his own stubborn self-will, he chose to go his own independent way and fellowship with God was broken. This self-will, characterized by an attitude of active rebellion or passive indifference, is an evidence of what the Bible calls sin.

Man Is Separated

"The wages of sin is death" [spiritual separation from God] (Romans 6:23, NASB).

God is holy and man is sinful. A great chasm separates the two. Men are continually trying to reach God and the abundant life through their own efforts: good life, ethics, philosophy, and more.

HOLY GOD

SINFUL PEOPLE

The Third Law gives us the only answer to this dilemma. . .

LAW THREE

JESUS CHRIST IS GOD'S **ONLY** PROVISION FOR MAN'S SIN. THROUGH HIM YOU CAN KNOW AND EXPERIENCE GOD'S LOVE AND PLAN FOR YOUR LIFE.

He Died in Our Place

"God demonstrates His own love toward us, in that while we were yet sinners, Christ died for us" (Romans 5:8, NASB).

He Rose From the Dead

"Christ died for our sins. . .He was buried . . .He appeared to Cephas, then to the twelve. After that He appeared to more than five hundred..." (1 Corinthians 15:3-6, NASB).

He Is the Only Way to God

"Jesus said to him, 'I am the way, and the truth, and the life; no one comes to the Father, but through Me'" (John 14:6, NASB).

God has bridged the chasm which separates us from Him by sending His Son, Jesus Christ, to die on the cross in our place.

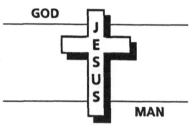

LAW FOUR

WE MUST INDIVIDUALLY **RECEIVE** JESUS CHRIST AS SAVIOR AND LORD; THEN WE CAN KNOW AND EXPERIENCE GOD'S LOVE AND PLAN FOR OUR LIVES.

We Must Receive Christ

"As many as received Him, to them He gave the right to become children of God, even to those who believe in His name" (John 1:12, NASB).

We Receive Christ Through Faith

"By grace you have been saved through faith; and that not of yourselves, it is the gift of God; not as a result of works, that no one should boast" (Ephesians 2:8,9, NASB).

We Receive Christ Through Personal Invitation

"Behold, I stand at the door and knock; if any one hears My voice and opens the door, I will come in to him" (Revelation 3:20, NASB).

Receiving Christ involves turning to God from self, trusting Christ to come into our lives to forgive our sins and make us what He wants us to be. It is not enough to give intellectual assent to His claims or to have an emotional experience.

These two circles represent two kinds of lives:

SELF-DIRECTED LIFE

S—Self is on the throne

†—Christ is outside the life

●—Interests are directed by self, often resulting in discord and frustration

27

CHRIST-DIRECTED LIFE

†—Christ is in the life and on the throne

S—Self is yielding to Christ

●—Interests are directed by Christ, resulting in harmony with God's plan

Which circle represents your life?

Which circle would you like to have represent your life?

The following explains how you can receive Christ:

YOU CAN RECEIVE CHRIST RIGHT NOW THROUGH PRAYER

(Prayer is talking with God)

God knows your heart and is not so concerned with your words as He is with the attitude of your heart. The following is a suggested prayer:

Lord Jesus, I need You. I open the door of my life and receive You as my Savior and Lord. Thank You for forgiving my sins. Take control of the throne of my life. Make me the kind of person You want me to be.

Does this prayer express the desire of your heart?

If it does, pray this prayer right now, and Christ will come into your life, as He promised.

How to Know If Christ Is in Your Life

Did you receive Christ into your life? According to His promise in Revelation 3:20, where is Christ right now in relation to you? Christ said that He would come into your life. Would He mislead you? On what authority do you know that God has answered your prayer? (The trust-worthiness of God Himself and His Word).

The Bible Promises Eternal Life to All Who Receive Christ

"The witness is this, that God has given us eternal life, and this life is in His Son. He who has the Son has the life; he who does not have the Son of God does not have the life. These things I have written to you who believe in the name of the Son of God, in order that you may know that you have eternal life" (1 John 5:11-13, NASB).

Thank God often that Christ is in your life and that He will never leave you.[2] You can know the living Christ indwells you, and that you have eternal life, from the very moment you invite Him in on the basis of His promise. He will not deceive you.

[2]Hebrews 13:5.

Response Form

☐ Please send me more information on how I can become a Christian.

☐ I have just received Jesus Christ as my Savior and would appreciate more information on how to experience the abundant Christian life.

☐ Please send me a *free* catalog of other books, booklets, audio cassettes, and videos by Bill Bright.

_____
NAME

_____
ADDRESS

_____
CITY

_____
STATE   ZIP

Please check the appropriate box(es) and mail this form in an envelope to:

> Bill Bright
> Campus Crusade for Christ
> P.O. Box 593684
> Orlando, FL 32859